Who's Who In

PEOPLESTOWN

Historic Edition

Who's Who In
PEOPLESTOWN
Atlanta, GA

Historic Edition

ThomasMax

TM

Your Publisher
For The 21st Century

Cover design by Lee Clevenger
Edited by Ellen N. Fleming
Front cover photo by A. Mustafa Ali
Photo of Turner Field by Lanard Cullins
History of Peoplestown by Larry Keating and Lauren Keating

ISBN Number 978-0-9788571-8-9
First printing, March 2008

Published by:

ThomasMax Publishing
P.O. Box 250054
Atlanta, GA 30325
www.thomasmax.com

TABLE OF CONTENTS

ACKNOWLEDGEMENTS

A warm thank you to:

Our Unveiling Event Sponsors who supported the publication of this book: Washington Mutual, The Annie E, Casey Foundation, Smith Real Estates Services, The Center for Working Families, Enterprise Community Partner, Inc., Council Person Mary Norwood and Donald Trimble Mortuary, Inc.

.

Our Ad and Patron contributors who supported the publication of this book.

All of the participants who worked on the various PRC Committees: Loretta Barnes, Sheryl Bennett, Sherise Brown, Lee Clevenger (Thomas Max Publishing), Lanard Cullins, George Epps, Ellen N. Fleming, Samuel Fountain, Forrest Gibson, Clemmie Jenkins, Larry Keating, Deborah Minor, Marilyn Simmons, and Columbus Ward, Jr.

The Peoplestown Community.

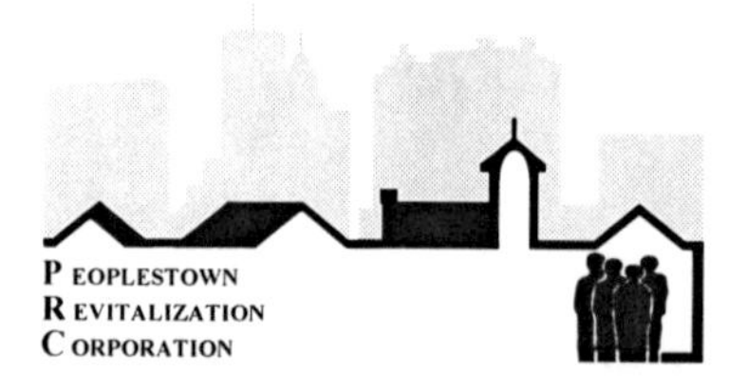

FROM THE PRESIDENT

Greetings:

Peoplestown Revitalization Corporation (PRC) is proud to provide this book as a fundraising initiative to support projects impacting the Peoplestown Community. One of our focus areas is to improve the quality of life for the residents through our initiatives to revitalize the community through housing development, economic development and community development. We are concerned about our young people and continue to seek ways to sustain our neighborhoods as we pursue job creation opportunities. We continue to pursue a safe and crime free neighborhood through finding ways to fund relevant projects and programs in the community.

Our mission is:
"To improve the quality of life for residents of our community, with emphasis on low-income residents, through, but not limited to, economic empowerment, residents development and rehabilitation (including affordable low-income housing) and any other activity that will enhance or better the community and empower our residents."

Having the opportunity to produce this book provides us with a written document as a way to preserve the history of the Peoplestown Community.

On behalf of Peoplestown Revitalization Corporation and the PRC Board of Directors, I would like to thank you for your support.

Columbus Ward, Jr.
President
Peoplestown Revitalization Corporation

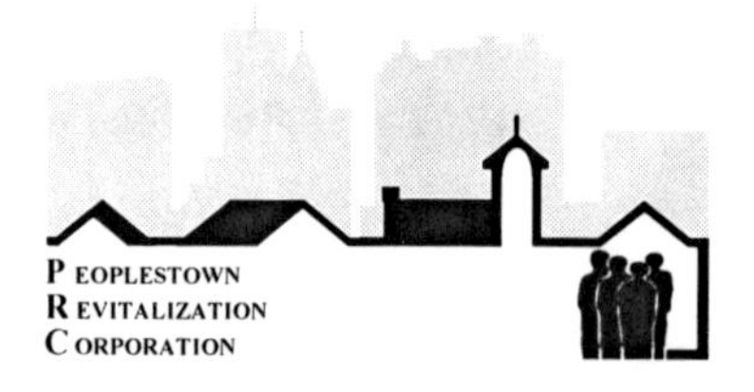

FROM THE EDITOR:

Greetings to our readers:

For the past 14 years, Peoplestown Revitalization Corporation (PRC) has been one of the leading Community Development Corporations (CDCs) which has continued to focus on its mission to revitalize the Peoplestown Community while improving the quality life for its residents. We have a rich history of impacting the Peoplestown Neighborhood through housing development, community development and economic development.

On behalf of Peoplestown Revitalization Corporation, I would like to thank you for purchasing this book in support of our fundraising initiative. Your involvement, through the purchase of the book, will add value to educating our community and others on the revitalization and evolution of a renewal community through efforts of a Community Development Corporation.

PRC is pleased to present "Who's Who in Peoplestown-Historic Edition", which reflects those who have laid the foundation for growth in the past, allowing us to achieve the current progress of development in Peoplestown today. Future publications will be done annually to continue to reflect our progress and provide a continual documentary for years to come. The publication and sales of this book will support our initiative to provide several scholarships to eligible Peoplestown Youth, support a Peoplestown Senior Educational Development Event, as well as support PRC Operational needs.

It is our desire that this book becomes the first of many educational documents that promotes continual change initiatives to other Community Development Corporations seeking to preserve their history.

Dr. Ellen N. Fleming, Editor
CEO/Executive Director
Peoplestown Revitalization Corporation

Peoplestown Revitalization Corporation
Board of Directors

Mr. Jared Bagby

Ms. Loretta Barnes

Ms. Lou Ann Braxton

Mr. Dana Chestnut

Mr. Robert Dudley

Mr. Samuel Fountain

Mrs. Clemmie Jenkins

Ms. May Helen Johnson

Mr. Larry Keating

Mr. William McFarland

Ms. Marilyn Simmons

Dr. Thomas Simmons, Jr.

Mr. Columbus Ward, Jr.

Letters From Officials

STATE OF GEORGIA

OFFICE OF THE GOVERNOR

ATLANTA 30334-0900

Sonny Perdue
GOVERNOR

August 8, 2007

Dear Friends:

It is a pleasure to send greetings at the first annual Unveiling Event for the publication of the *Who's Who in Peoplestown – Historic Edition*. This is truly a grand occasion.

For the past fourteen years, and as one of Georgia's finest Community Development Corporations, the Peoplestown Revitalization Corporation has continued to focus on its mission to revitalize the community through housing, community and economic development.

Focusing on the History of Peoplestown, Investor and Partnerships and the Next Generation, the *Who's Who in Peoplestown – Historic Edition*, will serve as the first in an ongoing series reflecting Peopletown's progress and the growth of a sustainable community.

We appreciate the Peoplestown Community's many contributions to Georgia's success and extend our best wishes on this special occasion.

Sincerely,

Sonny Perdue

CITY OF ATLANTA

SHIRLEY FRANKLIN
MAYOR

55 TRINITY AVE. S.W
ATLANTA, GEORGIA 30335-0300

TEL (404) 330-6100

August 18, 2007

Greetings,

As Mayor of Atlanta, it is my pleasure to congratulate Peoplestown Revitalization Corporation (PRC) for celebrating the history of the Peoplestown Community through the unveling of its book, "*Who's Who In Peoplestown – Historic Edition*".

This valuable publication serves as a way of educating our communities and others of those who have laid the foundation for growth in the past and created the pathway for achievements that helped shaped Peoplestown today. Peoplestown Revitalization Corporation has been one of the established Community Development Corporations (CDCs) which has continued to focus on its mission to revitalize the Peoplestown Community while improving the quality of life for its residents.

Peoplestown Revitalization Corporation has helped to develop a rich history in the evolution of this renewal community through housing development, community development and economic development. The City of Atlanta commends you as you celebrate a portion of Atlanta's history through the unveiling of this publication.

Sincerely

Shirley Franklin

Shirley Franklin

ATLANTA CITY COUNCIL

CARLA SMITH
COUNCILMEMBER
DISTRICT ONE

55 TRINITY AVENUE, S.W
SECOND FLOOR, EAST
ATLANTA, GEORGIA 303
(404) [illegible]

August 8, 2007

Greetings,

It is always a pleasure to celebrate history. As the Council Member of District One I congratulate the Peoplestown Revitalization Corporation (PRC) and the publication of "Who's Who in Peoplestown-Historic Edition". This book and its future editions will help preserve the history of this community and document its contribution to the City of Atlanta.

It has been my pleasure to serve the residents of Peoplestown and to assist the Peoplestown Revitalization Corporation in the efforts to revitalize the Peoplestown community through their housing and community economic development initiatives. Peoplestown Revitalization Corporation (PRC) is one of the Community Development Corporations (CDCs) which has maintained their mission to revitalize the Peoplestown Community while improving the quality of life for its residents.

On behalf of the residents of District One, congratulations and best wishes on this memorable occasion.

Sincerely,

Carla Smith

Council Member,
Carla Smith

House of Representatives

MARGARET KAISER
REPRESENTATIVE, DISTRICT 59
504 HILL STREET
ATLANTA, GEORGIA 30812
(404) 656-0274 (O)
(404)-223-6269 (H)
(404) 288-6049 (FAX)
EMAIL: margaret.kaiser@house.ga.gov

COVERDELL LEGISLATIVE OFFICE BLDG., ROOM 604
ATLANTA, GEORGIA 30334
(404) 656-0265
(404) 463-2634 (FAX)

STANDING
COMMITTEES:

BANKS & BANKING
EDUCATION
HEALTH & HUMAN SERVICES
INDUISTRIAL RELATIONS

September 20, 2007

As the State Legislator for House District 59, I could not be more excited to represent the citizens of the diverse and ever-changing community of Peoplestown. As one of the Stadium neighborhoods, the area is not only rich in history, but rich in leadership and community activism. It is my distinct pleasure and privilege to be able to participate with the citizens of Summerhill to help continue to bring about positive change in this community. I am honored to be a part of this program recognizing Who's Who in Peoplestown.

Yours truly,

Rep. Margaret Kaiser

BOARD OF COMMISSIONERS OF FULTON COUNTY

FULTON COUNTY GOVERNMENT CENTER
141 PRYOR STREET, SW
ATLANTA, GEORGIA 30303

Robert L. "Robb" Pitts
COMMISSIONER

August 3, 2007

Dr. Ellen N. Flemming
CEO/Executive Director
Peoplestown Revitalization Corporation
1044 Washington St. Suite I
Atlanta, GA 30315

Dear Dr. Flemming:

Congratulations on the publication of "Who's Who in Peoplestown-Historic Edition" and for providing 14 years of successful service to the Peoplestown community. Peoplestown Revitalization Corporation has enhanced the quality of life for its residents and neighbors through successful housing, community and economic development.

Your positive impact on the community is to be commended. I wish you the best on your future revitalization efforts.

Keep up the great work!

Sincerely,

Robb Pitts

LISA M. BORDERS
PRESIDENT

ATLANTA CITY COUNCIL

55 TRINITY AVENUE, S.W.
SUITE 2900
ATLANTA, GEORGIA 30303
Main (404) 330-[illegible]
Fax (404) 658-7551
Email lmborders@atlantaga.gov

August 8, 2007

Greetings:

I want to extend heartfelt greetings and congratulations to the Peoplestown Revitalization Corporation as we celebrate the history of the Peoplestown Community through the unveiling of the book, "Who's Who In Peoplestown-Historic Edition.

Since it's founding, the Peoplestown Revitalization Corporation has continued to focus on its mission to revitalize the Peoplestown Community, while improving the quality of life for its residents. The Peoplestown Revitalization Corporation has helped to develop a rich history in the evolution of this renewal community through economic development.

On behalf of the City of Atlanta and the Atlanta City Council, I commend you as you celebrate Atlanta's history, and extend best wishes for your continued success.

Sincerely,

Lisa M. Borders
President
Atlanta City Council

Peoplestown . . . a historical perspective

History of Peoplestown

EARLY HISTORY: A STREETCAR SUBURB

Peoplestown was developed as a streetcar suburb after the Atlantic Electric Railway built a line along Capitol Avenue (now Hank Aaron Drive) in 1885. Typical of Atlanta and the South, the development that followed was composed of middle- and upper-class Victorian homes as well as small, modest homes. It contained both racially integrated sections and an enclave of exclusively black residences. Victorian homes for upper- and middle-class whites were built along streets and avenues with rail or streetcar service. These streets were both paved and wider than the streets in the neighborhood's interior east of Capitol Avenue. Alleys divided each block and provided separate access for black households, who lived in small shacks at the rear of many lots.

South of Atlanta Avenue and east of Capitol Avenue, narrower unpaved streets and smaller lots marked the location of a black enclave. The Peeples family, possible namesakes of the neighborhood, owned 66 lots in this section, just as it was beginning to develop in 1894. Some older residents remember the name as the Peoples family. The name Peeples came from insurance maps.

By 1925, insurance maps showed 550 residences (510 single-family homes and 40 in duplex structures). Because homes in Peoplestown's black enclave were not shown, these figures represent only the white and internally integrated portions of Peoplestown. Grace Barksdale, a 70-year resident of Peoplestown's black enclave, described neighborhood life in the 1930s:

"There wasn't anybody had a street. It was like wagon trails . . . . Started paving in the '30s. We had electricity on Martin Street. We did not have it running down here. We did not have no gas. So I got them gas. And it was so dark down here, I got them to give me light. It was in the '30s, about '36 or '37. We weren't getting far, but you was getting paved streets."

The 1920s and '30s also brought significant change to the white portions of Peoplestown. When the upper classes began to commute in automobiles, they also began to move north along Peachtree Street. Middle-class development followed. As a consequence, demand for the less-prestigious southside streetcar suburbs declined.

A GROWING BLACK COMMUNITY

The 1939 Works Progress Administration Real Property Survey provides the first clear picture of the black enclave on Peoplestown's east side: The 12 blocks east of Violet, west of Hill, south of Vanaria and north of Boynton were almost 100% black. The proportion of renters in this section was 33%. Overall, Peoplestown had 1,159 housing units with 792 (68%) rental units, 367 (32%) owner-occupied units, 188 (16%) black-occupied units and 971 (84%) white-occupied units.

Many black residents gathered together to lobby for a neighborhood school. After the initial rejection of the school proposal, Henry and Louise Phipps, Grace Barksdale, Sarah Baker (who operated Mama Baker's Nursery), Rev. L.W. and Myrtice Hope, Loretta Barnes, Ollie M. Powell, Miss Christine and other residents formed the Peoplestown Civic League in 1953 or '54. The next attempt succeeded, and D.H. Stanton Elementary School opened in 1958, with J.Y. Moreland as principal.

Mrs. Powell suggested naming the school after Daniel Hector Stanton, a respected Atlanta minister who provided spiritual inspiration to the community. Mrs. Barnes served as the first president of the Parent Teacher Association. Under Mrs. Barnes' leadership, the school won the Milk Bowel Trophy for two consecutive years. She also led the adult literacy program.

Phipps describes the community in the 1950s:

"After we got the gas and the street paved, and the school and the park, everything looked good. Most everybody owned their houses down in here. . . . We used to do our shopping on Georgia Avenue. They had a big supermarket there. They had a chicken house there and they sold chicken and fish. And then they had a theater on the corner of Crew Street and Georgia Avenue. Then below that they had a shoe shop, a bakery and on the other side of the street they had Fritz's Ice Cream. They used to have a grocery store up there at Violet and Haygood."

Ethel Mae Mathews described the neighborhood at about the same time: "Peoplestown was a people's town. Rich Jews, poor blacks, rich, white, just mixed in together. We had drugstores, grocery stores, a theater."

The next reliable data point regarding Peoplestown's racial composition is the 1960 census block data. The number of housing units had increased to 1,509, with 751 (49.8%) black-occupied units and 758 (50.2%) white-occupied units. Whites still lived on the west side of the neighborhood and blacks on the east side. The total population was 6,831.

OUTSIDE INFLUENCES

Unfortunately, 1960 marked an apex in Peoplestown's

Georgia Railway and Power
The 975 is on Atlanta Avenue near Grant Park

ATS 1831 was one of the last group of trolley coaches purchased by Georgia Power Company. It was built in 1948 and is shown here on Georgia Avenue at Prior Street during expressway construction demolition on March 20, 1958. *Photo by Bill Volkmer.*

development. During the next 30 years, a succession of local, state and federal government and private business initiatives undermined the tenuous stability that the lower-middle-class and poor neighborhood had attained.

Atlanta's plans for highway construction substantially affected Peoplestown's future development. But Peoplestown almost escaped unscathed. An initial proposal called for the primary north-south expressway to circumnavigate the Central Business District (CBD) on the west side. This alignment would have brought the expressway well west of Peoplestown.

The location of highways, however, is driven by land use as well as transportation goals. At the behest of Central Area Improvement Association and then-Mayor William Hartsfield's administration, the downtown connector's location was shifted to the east side of the central area, where it could accomplish several tasks: removing parts of three neighborhoods occupied by low-income black residents, separating the central area from two public housing communities, and serving as a buffer between the central area and residual portions of black neighborhoods.

The realignment moved the expressway's route to Peoplestown. In the early 1960s, Interstate 75/85 sliced off the west side of the neighborhood, demolishing 110 primarily single-family units, separating Peoplestown from the Pittsburgh neighborhood, and setting the stage for a sequence of urban renewal, Model Cities and stadium construction programs.

While the initial damage to Peoplestown from the expressway was an *indirect* consequence of destructive local transportation and land use polices aimed at other poor black communities, the urban renewal program *intentionally* brought the same set of local policies to

Peoplestown's borders. The Washington-Rawson urban renewal project implemented the city policy of demolishing low-income black neighborhoods surrounding the CBD in the southeast quadrant of the intersection of the east-west and north-south expressways, three blocks north of Peoplestown.

The initial 1957 plan and legal justification for the Washington-Rawson project was to replace more than 1,000 low-income black-occupied housing units with moderate-income ownership housing, light industry, businesses, schools and parks. Part of the project's rationale was to redevelop the area as a buffer between Peoplestown, Summerhill and the CBD.

In the early phases of urban renewal, only property owners were paid relocation expenses. Plans for acquisition and demolition were kept as secret as possible. Mrs. Mathews was a renter in the neighborhood during this period, and she recalls that officials came to her home and ordered her to move within weeks.

THE FIRST STADIUM

In spring 1963, plans for the area abruptly changed. According to then-Mayor Ivan Allen Jr., he spontaneously conceived of a stadium on the urban renewal land at a poignant last moment, in order to convince Kansas City Athletics owner Charles O. Finley not to end his secret visit to the city with diminished impressions of Atlanta as the location for his major league baseball team. A more prosaic and probably accurate version of the story says Allen located the stadium at the Washington-Rawson site to thwart black community proposals for black public housing there. Stadium planning and design began within six weeks of Allen's meeting with Finley. The privately controlled Atlanta-Fulton County Recreation Authority (the legal entity designed to build and manage the stadium) paid insufficient attention to certain technical details which, properly handled, could have partially protected Peoplestown, Summerhill and Mechanicsville from the stadium's negative impacts.

The Milwaukee Braves agreed to move to Atlanta in February 1964, and it negotiated the provision of an additional 2,500 parking spaces by the city within 10 years of the team's 1966 arrival.

The stadium had a capacity of 55,000 people. When the stadium was full, 12,462 cars had to find parking. After 1976, the 6,600 formal, public sector parking spaces provided room for a little more than one-half the cars. The remaining cars parked in the surrounding residential areas. The land-use consequence of this approach was that the first two to three blocks surrounding the stadium had almost all their houses burned down or demolished to create informal sector or "gypsy" parking. This land lay empty, vacant and dangerous on non-game nights. The two- and three-block band of vacant land encircling the stadium was immune to development and retarded development farther into the neighborhoods' interior for more than 25 years.

The event transportation plan equally disregarded Peoplestown, Summerhill and Mechanicsville's interests. It stipulated that all major streets in the three neighborhoods would be converted to one-way streets carrying traffic into the stadium area for one and one-half hours prior to a game, and they would be converted to one-way streets carrying traffic away from the stadium for more than an hour after the game. To leave their neighborhoods before a game against the flow of traffic and going the wrong way on a one-way street, residents describe a process involving trying to guess which police officer would not chase them down. Reaching their homes from outside the neighborhood after a game was simply impossible in a car.

Demolition of the area immediately north of Peoplestown produced two additional negative impacts. First, the commercial district along Georgia Avenue described earlier by Henry Phipps was demolished. The supermarket, theater, bakery and other commercial businesses had served Peoplestown and nearby neighborhoods for more than 25 years.

Second, the destruction of more than 1,000 low-income housing units -- coupled with a citywide housing policy that demolished at least 14,000 more low-income units than it replaced -- exacerbated substandard housing conditions.

Resistance to widespread demolition festered in the neighborhoods around the stadium. Atlanta's most publicized riot during the 1960s occurred on the Tuesday after Labor Day in 1966 and centered at Capitol Avenue and Ormond Street. Housing conditions headed the list of grievances that neighborhood representatives reported to Mayor Allen in the riot's aftermath.

In the spring after the riot, Rev. Austin Ford founded Emmaus House, which operates a community action center that helped catalyze organizing in Peoplestown and political action on Model Cities, highways and stadiums, among other issues.

After the riot, local policy appeared to shift — at least on the surface. The Allen administration set a goal of 17,000 new low- and moderate-income housing units. Relocation housing and repair of existing housing were identified as priorities. Peoplestown, Summerhill and Mechanicsville were included in the new Model Cities

The Old Atlanta-Fulton County Stadium

program area and grassroots participation was promised.

But promises exceeded capacities and political will. The Model Cities plan targeted the district south of Georgia Avenue and north of Peoplestown as one of the three Economic Growth Cases intended to produce "high quality commercial and residential development." Over consistent neighborhood opposition emanating from Emmaus House and the Poverty Rights Office, which included a November 1970 "sleep-in" in the Model Cities Director's office led by Mrs. Mathews, the area was cleared and became the locus of most of the 2,500 stadium parking spaces promised to the baseball team. In 1991, it became the proposed site of the new Olympic Stadium.

Peoplestown did gain some new low- to moderate-income housing during this era. Eighty-seven units were built just north of the neighborhood on Washington and Crew streets. A non-profit corporation formed by Emmaus House and Peoplestown residents acted as the conduit for two rental developments, Capital Vanaria (60 units) and Boynton Village (43 units) in 1978.

HIGHWAY INTRUSION

In the 1970s, the Atlanta Regional Commission and the Georgia Department of Transportation proposed the reconstruction and widening of I-75/I-85 on the west side of Peoplestown.

The proposal envisioned widening the expressway from six to 10 lanes. It called for the demolition of about 50 residences and 15 businesses in Peoplestown. Also, it would have eliminated several hundred parking spaces between Peoplestown and the stadium.

Grassroots resistance focused on the homes and businesses slated for demolition. Emmaus House, Mrs. Mathews and others pressed for minimal relocation and equitable treatment of relocatees. This resistance did achieve a 55-unit reduction in the total number of demolished units, and relocation payments for some displaced residents.

The I-75/85 expressway was reconfigured and rebuilt by 1988. Peoplestown lost four city blocks to the widening. Reorganization of interstate interchanges forced more event traffic through the neighborhood. The loss of formal parking increased pressure for the informal parking lots to push deeper into the northern section of Peoplestown.

While the neighborhood fought external threats, community members strengthened the ties that bind. In 1990, Clemmie C. Jenkins, Cecilia O'Kelly, Rufus O'Kelly and others started the Peoplestown Reunion on the third weekend of September. The reunion takes place annually, and it draws many people who have moved away from the neighborhood back to enjoy the company of neighbors who still live in Peoplestown.

In the late 1980s, national foundations that supported nonprofit community development corporations made a second attempt to connect with vigorous neighborhood organizations in Atlanta. In 1988, Massachusetts Institute of Technology and the Ford Foundation identified Atlanta as the largest American city without CDCs. A major blockage had been the local business community's hostility toward autonomous neighborhood institutions; these antipathies were expressed to national foundations and had undermined their initial interest.

Simultaneously, Peoplestown activists were gathering support to explore alternatives for community-based development. Columbus Ward, Father Ford and Gene Bowen solicited support from the Welfare Rights Organization led by Mrs. Mathews, the Peoplestown Civic League, the Peoplestown Reunion Group, and the Peoplestown Advisory Board (an outgrowth of a Model Cities organization supported by Economic Opportunity Atlanta). The three organizers connected with the AMOCO Foundation, which agreed to fund workshops on the roles, responsibilities, organization and accomplishments of community-based CDCs. Most people participating in these meetings were enthusiastic about the prospect of a neighborhood-directed development organization playing a leading role in Peoplestown's redevelopment. Since residents had been historically excluded from decisions on urban renewal, expressways, stadiums, parking and Model Cities programs - and only gained any influence over the program's effects through tenacious activism -- the prospect of increased community control over development offered clear advantages.

Thomas Simmons joined Ward as a central actor in the formation of the Peoplestown Revitalization Corporation (PRC). Many neighborhood civic activists (Mrs. Mathews, Marilyn Simmons, Robert Dudley, Willam Teasley, Gene Fergeson, May Helen Johnson and Lou Ann Braxton) played vigorously constructive roles. AMOCO provided seed money for incorporation as a 501(c)3 nonprofit in 1990, culminating several years of organizing efforts.

Among the first staff were Wendy Scruggs Murray and Gwendolyn Burson. William McFarland was hired to work on housing issues and eventually, after an apprenticeship under Ward's direction, he became executive director. As PRC matured and became more effective, John Armour was hired as the lead housing staff.

NEW STADIUM THREAT

Very little is publicly known about the internal dynamics of Atlanta's bid preparation process for the 1996 Olympic Games. The secret negotiations led to a proposal to build an Olympic Stadium, then convert it into a new baseball stadium for the Atlanta Braves and to locate that stadium south of the existing facility.

Columbus Ward, Mrs. Mathews, Duane Stuart and others formed Atlanta Neighborhoods United for Fairness (A'NUFF) to resist the Olympic Stadium proposal in October 1990, immediately after Atlanta was awarded the 1996 Olympics and the proposed new Olympic Stadium just north of Peoplestown was officially announced.

A'NUFF opposed the stadium because the surrounding neighborhoods had been forced to absorb traffic, parking and noise impacts from the existing stadium for 20 years. The group called for a publicly accessible planning process to determine whether a new stadium was needed and environmental impact analyses of multiple potential sites.

In early December, the editor of *The Atlanta Constitution's* editorial pages interpreted A'NUFF's opposition to a second stadium as much more politically threatening opposition to the Olympic Games themselves. Tom Teepen editorialized that " . . . their representatives are swearing simply to keep the games from occurring at all."

Mathews and Stuart retorted that they were not opposed to the Olympics, only to the stadium. They replied: "This trivializes the intent of those who are against the building of the second stadium. The issues here are not so simplistic. Twenty-five years of urban renewal, stadium building and highway construction have served to maintain this area as an underdeveloped enclave in the shadow of downtown."

Throughout the winter and spring of 1991, A'NUFF picketed Olympic organizer Billy Payne's Dunwoody home and worked to develop allies in the labor movement and other neighborhoods. By July 1991, A'NUFF had convinced leaders of other Neighborhood Planning Units to adopt a draft plan calling for the Olympic Stadium to be built elsewhere. The Atlanta Planning Advisory Board (APAB), composed of the presidents of Atlanta's 24 NPUs, suggested either that Georgia Tech's 45,000-seat Grant Field be used for the Olympics (Grant Field did not have any Olympic sporting events scheduled), or that two other sites be considered for a new stadium.

At the end of the summer, the Atlanta Committee for the Olympic Games (AGOC), the City of Atlanta and

Fulton County reached a preliminary agreement on some stadium issues. Most importantly from Peoplestown's perspective, the site of the proposed stadium was moved one-quarter mile north, almost adjacent to the existing stadium. A'NUFF's protests and political pressure had succeeded in moving the stadium a short distance away from the neighborhood.

During the winter and spring of 1991, the Community Design Center of Atlanta (CDCA) worked on a redevelopment plan for Peoplestown and a study of Olympic impacts in six neighborhoods most likely to be affected by the event and associated construction.

When presented with CDCA's recommendation that the neighborhoods seek 12,500 parking spaces if they were backed into accepting one of the stadiums, Ward wisely said, "We should seek 13,500 spaces in order to provide some security for the neighborhoods."

But, a united neighborhood position advocating the 13,500 parking spaces that would have been sufficient to take the pressure of gypsy lots off the surrounding communities was not politically possible. Summerhill had broken ranks with Peoplestown and Mechanicsville when the Atlanta Committee for the Olympic Games, Central Atlanta Progress and Atlanta political leadership offered Summerhill substantial private investment, a hold on more parking (no parking east of Frasier Street), first place in neighborhood redevelopment planning line, and more than $50 million in public investment in exchange for backing the Olympic stadium and acting publicly as if it was the only neighborhood affected by its construction.

The remaining politically feasible path was to accept the city's offer of insufficient parking, fight between themselves about where it would go, and try to fend off gypsy parking in the future.

In September 1991, ACOG took its first formal steps to address neighborhood concerns by creating a "Neighborhood Task Force." It included Ward, the chair of NPU-V, and Mrs. Mathews.

The task force was temporarily disbanded after four secret meetings during the next six weeks. ACOG shrank the task force's mandate from "an active part in what goes on" to the compilation of a list of concerns (recorded and interpreted by ACOG staff).

Ward later said, "The Neighborhood Task Force was always a support group for ACOG. They called the meetings and the neighborhoods were always a minority."

In July 1992, the Braves and the Atlanta-Fulton County Recreation Authority reached an agreement for 10,000 parking places. The neighborhoods were assigned one small-possibly-to-be-built-in-the-future parking lot as the substitute for a community improvement fund, plus 25% of parking revenues from three annual events in the Braves' stadium.

Neighborhood reaction was swift. They rejected the offer. "We can't settle for this, considering the impact on our neighborhoods by the Braves," Ward said.

Two weeks later, the city increased the pressure on Peoplestown by effectively leaving the neighborhood out of the "Olympic Development Program" it presented to the International Olympic Committee (IOC) in Barcelona. Detailed budgets were presented for Summerhill, Vine City, Techwood and Mechanicsville, but Peoplestown had only a cryptic "costs to be determined" entry. The message was not lost on Ward. "The city periodically tried to pressure us into dropping our resistance to what they were doing," Ward said of the omission.

In September 1992, ACOG reconvened the

Neighborhood Task Force with an ultimatum to come up with a plan for the 10,000 parking spaces that the Braves demanded. On Sept. 16, a minority of the original 25-member task force voted 7-2 with five abstentions to approve a 10,000 parking space plan.

A corollary issue was whether union labor would be required on stadium construction. ACOG had taken an early, transparently anti-union position. The Atlanta Labor Council's initial call for union wages was modified to a possible willingness to accept "prevailing wages" (an average of union/non-union wages). The neighborhoods had responded to the Labor Council's proposals for job training programs for neighborhood people by endorsing the Labor Council wage position.

Parking, however, was still the central issue. Pressure to begin construction moved the parking negotiations to a conclusion in winter 1993. The parking plan was released to the public on Feb. 8. Peoplestown went 0 for 3: A new 351-space lot was slated to go two blocks into the neighborhood's interior; the city complained that there was little it could do to eliminate informal sector lots; and no physical buffers separating the stadium or parking from neighborhoods were proposed.

"We will not tolerate that type of behavior and disrespect," Ward said.

AGREEMENTS AND COMPROMISES

Then, the parking plan broke down over parking and fiscal issues. The interruption provided some political leverage for neighborhoods to push their agenda. In the end, the neighborhoods secured an important technical change to the community improvement fund: The 8.25% of *net* parking revenues the Braves had offered was changed to 8.25% of *gross* parking receipts, thus raising the fund in good years to approximately $300,000.

Another change promised "help" in raising an immediate $300,000, which was important because the fund would not begin generating revenues until 1997. Also, the proposed 351-space lot within Peoplestown was eliminated.

Peoplestown's vigilance and militancy did succeed in moving the stadium one-quarter mile north, in preserving a hospice and low-income housing development initially slated for demolition, in securing the demolition of the Atlanta-Fulton County Stadium, and in preventing the formal parking from intruding into the neighborhood. Also, Peoplestown's willingness to defend its interests in the face of hostile government and corporations created political space for other poor neighborhoods to press for compensatory resources and programs.

July brought the Olympic Stadium groundbreaking ceremonies and the prospect of substantial demonstrations against both the stadium and ACOG. The Atlanta Labor Council planned to join the neighborhoods in protesting the groundbreaking because ACOG had continuously rejected its requests to require union wages and benefits. But the night before the groundbreaking, contractors reached an agreement with the Atlanta Labor Council that set a wage floor of $7.50 an hour and specified wage rates for 18 construction crafts. Consequently, labor pulled out of the planned demonstrations, leaving the neighborhoods to carry on alone.

Members of A'NUFF constructed a tent city and conducted a vigil for two days prior to the ceremonies.

POST-OLYMPICS

Peoplestown continued to work consistently to protect and support its most vulnerable residents. PRC worked with many government and non-profit organizations to preserve, rehabilitate or build low- to moderate-income housing throughout the neighborhood. Along the northern boundary, PRC constructed a 94-unit low-income tax-credit development that includes some deeper subsidy homes as well. This community seals the border with the stadium to the north and blocks the intrusion of destructive informal-sector parking. Other developments in the neighborhood's interior focused on supplanting dehabilitating uses that undermined security: Along Fern Avenue, PRC redeveloped a string of duplexes that had been captured by drug pushers.

In attempts to contend with some of the multiple vulnerabilities that poverty entails, PRC has launched job training programs and neighborhood security systems. At the same time, PRC has maintained its close connections to Peoplestown's residents, fostering the participatory engagement that undergirds successful community development.

After the City of Atlanta failed to adopt and enforce effective prohibitions on informal-sector parking from stadium events, PRC organized indigenous enforcement patrols that have used blockades, trenches and other innovative approaches to preventing intrusions.

In 1997, The Atlanta-Fulton County Stadium was demolished. In recognition of decades of civic action, Mrs. Mathews helped push the button igniting the explosives. She said, "When I stood up there and helped blow up the old stadium, I felt I went down in history."

The original Olympic Stadium was built in a "bowl" configuration to house such events as track and field. Heavy reconstruction work was required to reconfigure the stadium for baseball's Atlanta Braves, which began playing their home games in renamed Turner Field in 1997.

(Turner Field photo below by Lanard Cullins)

FUTURE PROSPECTS

Successful groups of low-income black residents have tenaciously fought to build a stable community in Peoplestown. The first settlers constructed the nucleus of their community on the unpaved roads of the black enclave and in the shacks lining the alleys behind white residences. Mrs. Barksdale and other residents overcame Atlanta's institutional racism in the 1920s and '30s to obtain electricity, gas and paving of many streets. The Peoplestown Civic League led the fight for a school in the 1940s and '50s. From the 1960s onward, Mrs. Mathews, Columbus Ward, Gene Fergeson, Duane Stuart and others have fought nearly continuous battles against the destructive effects of expressways, urban renewal, Model Cities and stadiums.

More than 100 years of struggle have left Peoplestown damaged by the noxious land uses that surround it. Still, the neighborhood has remained tenacious in its battles to create a community that shelters its most vulnerable residents. Peoplestown's long history of political action has overcome many obstacles and outside forces, and those strengths should serve Peoplestown well in the future.

Revitalization-Past View

Revitalization-Present View

Revitalization - The Square At Peoplestown

Revitalization - Columbia At Peoplestown

Peoplestown
Youth on the Move Program

"Out of School Time Initiative"

Historical Background

...Then

The "Out of School Time" Initiative began as a pilot project in the summer of June 2003, which consisted of 14 Youth Advisory Board members, residing in the Peoplestown community. Majority of the youth were too old for summer camp and too young for employment and generally underserved. During that time, there were no programs that existed in Peoplestown or neighboring communities that targeted middle and high school youth. Thus, the Youth Advisory Board was developed to create a safe environment for students to convene, to create a platform where youth have a voice, to discuss needs specific to youth, and to formally bring these issues before the PRC board of directors.

Our Mission:

To expand the role of our youth in the revitalization of our community comprised of effective youth development activities that reflect the interest of the community's youth and encourages them to cultivate their leadership talents through activities that require a commitment to themselves and their community.

Objectives:

To support the youth in Peoplestown to successfully complete high school, access higher education, and/or obtain employment.

To have a measurable impact on participants by providing structured activities during non-school hours that will enhance their quality of life.

...Now

With the success of the program in its pilot stage, the initiative evolved into Peoplestown Youth on the Move, which is a community-based program located in the heart of the neighborhood and employs community residents. It is the only after-school initiative in the community that caters to ages 12-25. Middle school and high school students can take advantage of the resources that are available in their very own community.

The program staff consists of former and existing community residents with over 10 years of building relationships in the community. Since then, we have acquired a program director (full-time) and youth coordinator (part-time). Also, we have contracted staff and built numerous professional partnerships to provide support in the various program elements, to assist us in accomplishing our goals. Uniquely, YOM creates employment opportunities for eligible youth during the summer (ages 14-25), provides meaningful exposure/exploration experiences for program participants, exposure to multiple art forms, financial literacy, enhanced reading & math, health & fitness, tutorial assistance (with utilization of volunteers), activities that develop leadership, critical thinking, decision-making skills, and employ service learning.

Seven of fourteen original Youth Advisory Board members and some new recruits continue to serve as the governing body of the program. Regardless of the environmental challenges, our "Youth on the Move" participants' feel empowered and excited to attend school. Our enrichment opportunities give the youth a sense of confidence and inspire them to become excited about learning. We recognize that the confidence and skills that they acquire from participating in such activities are transferable to academic skills. Therefore, they perform better academically in school.

...To Date

100% of our students participating in YOM are promoted to the next grade level.
100% complete service learning projects and have a commitment to their community.
50% of the original members continue to serve on the Youth Advisory Board.
64% of the parents are involved in regular activities and events during the year.
60% (12 of 20 eligible students) have received job placement opportunities for consecutive years.

On behalf of Youth on the Move, we would like to extend a special thanks to PRC, United Way of Metropolitan Atlanta, the Yellowlees Family, St. Paul Foundation, the Enterprise Foundation, the McDevitt Youth Center and other sponsors for supporting youth initiatives in Peoplestown.

"The Next Generation"
Successful Youth of Peoplestown

Ashley Britt
Carver High School Graduate, 2005
Honor Student

David Blount
Carver High School Graduate, 2004
College Preparatory
Global Logistics Trainee Graduate, 2006

Joy Covington
Carver High School Graduate, 2003
Peoplestown Youth on the Move Program, 2003-
Culinary Arts Certification, Job Corp, 2005

Latonya Early
Southside High School Graduate
Honor Student
Hope Scholarship Recipient
Peoplestown Youth on the Move Program, 2003-
Registered Nursing Major, Georgia Perimeter College, 2007-

Alvin Garrett
Carver High School Graduate, 2004
Dual Diploma

Czjz Jones
The New Schools at Carver High Graduate, 2006

Carl Lane
Carver High School Graduate, 2004
Dual Diploma
Honor Student
Marine Corp, 2004-

Carlos Lane
Carver High School Graduate, 2004
Dual Diploma
Honor Student
Marine Corp, 2004-

Carlton Lane
Alpha Phi Alpha Scholarship Recipient
Physical Therapy Major, Atlanta Metropolitan College, 2004-

Shamika Lee
Southside High School Graduate, 2002

Rakia Reeves
Southside High School Graduate, 2002
Sociology Major, Savannah State College, 2003-

Shanteria Rivers
SIATech Graduate, 2006
Phoenix Award Recipient
Peoplestown Youth on the Move Program 2003-
Early Childhood Development Major, Atlanta Technical College, 2007-

Jamie Robinson
Grady High School Graduate, 2005
Peoplestown Youth on the Move Program 2003-
Graphic Design Dual Degree Program, Atlanta Technical College, 2004-2005
Graphic Design Major, Atlanta Technical College, 2005-

Adrian Strickland
Southside High School Graduate, 2002
Honor Student
Hope Scholarship Recipient
Perfect Attendance
Tuskegee Institute, 2002-03
Barbara-Scotia, 2003-2005

Rickey Taylor
Carver High School Graduate, 2004
Dual Diploma
Peoplestown Youth on the Move Program 2003-
Talladega College, 2004-2005

William Thurston, III
The New Schools at Carver High Graduate, 2006
National Honor Society
Honor Student
Project GRAD Atlanta Scholars
Hope Scholarship Recipient
Excellent Attendance
Peoplestown Youth on the Move Program 2003-
Journalism Major, Georgia Perimeter College, 2007-

Christopher Webb
The New Schools at Carver High Graduate, 2006
Salutatorian
National Honor Society
Top 10 Percent
Honor Student
Gifted and Talented
Project GRAD Atlanta Scholars
21st Century Underground Railroad Participant
Perfect Attendance 2005-2006
Valdosta State College, 2006-

Hassan Wilkins
Douglass High School Graduate, 2002
Marine Corp. Reserve, 2002-
Albany State University

In Appreciation and Special Recognition to …

PLATINUM LEVEL SPONSORS

Washington Mutual (WaMu)

The Annie E. Casey Foundation – Atlanta Civic Site

BRONZE LEVEL SPONSOR

Council Person Mary Norwood

Donald Trimble Mortuary, Inc.

Enterprise Community Partners, Inc.

Smith Real Estate Services

The Center for Working Families

Platinum Level Sponsors

Bronze Level Sponsors

Congratulations to PRC on your historic edition of Who's Who In Peoplestown

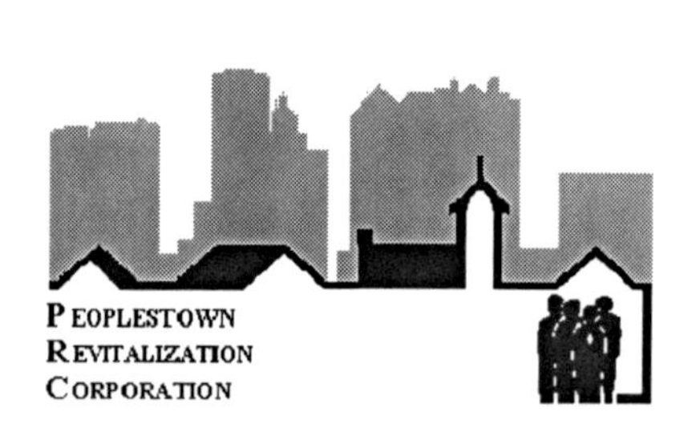

PRC gives special thanks to our sponsors!

Additional Supporters

Atlanta Housing Association of Neighborhood-based Developers

The Atlanta Housing Association of Neighborhood-based Developers (AHAND) is a trade association of Community Development Corporations committed to improving the quality of life in Atlanta's disenfranchised neighborhoods through economic development, affordable housing development and special services

AHAND Neighborhood-based Member

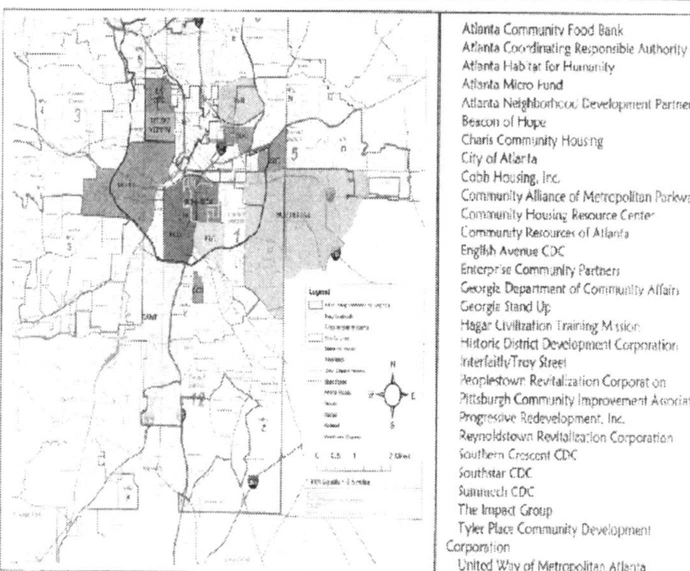

Member Organizations

Atlanta Community Food Bank
Atlanta Coordinating Responsible Authority
Atlanta Habitat for Humanity
Atlanta Micro Fund
Atlanta Neighborhood Development Partnership
Beacon of Hope
Charis Community Housing
City of Atlanta
Cobb Housing, Inc.
Community Alliance of Metropolitan Parkway
Community Housing Resource Center
Community Resources of Atlanta
English Avenue CDC
Enterprise Community Partners
Georgia Department of Community Affairs
Georgia Stand Up
Hagar Civilization Training Mission
Historic District Development Corporation
Interfaith/Troy Street
Peoplestown Revitalization Corporation
Pittsburgh Community Improvement Association
Progressive Redevelopment, Inc.
Reynoldstown Revitalization Corporation
Southern Crescent CDC
Southstar CDC
Summech CDC
The Impact Group
Tyler Place Community Development Corporation
United Way of Metropolitan Atlanta

Special thanks to our sponsors and partners:

Washington Mutual

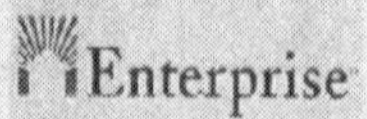

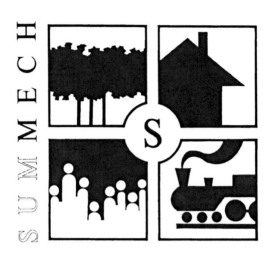

ATLANTA CITY COUNCIL

CEASAR C. MITCHELL
COUNCILMEMBER
POST 1 AT-LARGE

55 TRINITY AVENUE, S.W.
SECOND FLOOR EAST
ATLANTA, GEORGIA 30335
DIRECT (404) 330-6052
MAIN (404) 330-6030
FAX (404) 658-6562
E-MAIL CCMITCHELL@ATLANTAGA.GOV
WWW.CEASARMITCHELL.COM

July 20, 2007

Dear Members of the Peoplestown Revitalization Corporation.

Congratulations on your inaugural publication of *Who's Who in Peoplestown – Historical Edition.*

I am anxious to see the finished work and I look forward to sharing the good practices with other thriving communities.

If I or my office can be of assistance to you, please do not hesitate to contact me at (404) 330-6052.

Yours in Service,

Ceasar C. Mitchell

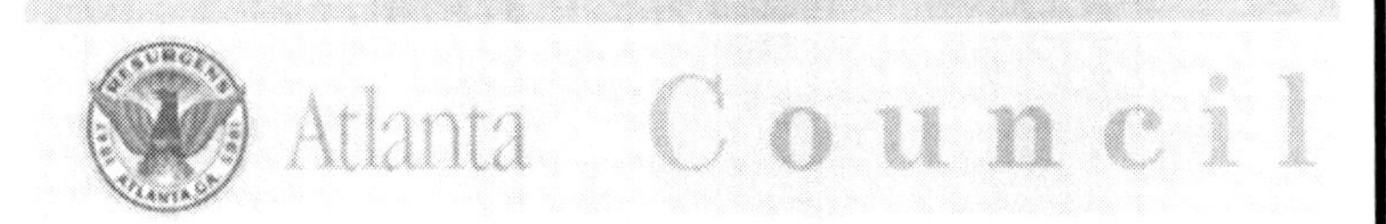

Atlanta City Council member
Carla Smith
Atlanta City Hall
55 Trinity Avenue, SW
Suite 2900
Atlanta, Georgia 30303
404-330-6039
csmith@atlantaga.gov
www.district1atlanta.com

2007 City Committee Assignments
•**City Utilities**, chairwoman
•Public Safety
•Zoning

District 1 Staff
Sheryl Bennett, Community Liaison
Brenda Hampton, Constituent Services
Preya Grover, Administrative Support

Congratulations

Peoplestown Revitalization Corporation
on the publication of
"Who's Who in Peoplestown-Historic Edition"

Congratulations and much success on the first annual

" Who's Who in Peoplestown – Historic Edition "

Nancy A. Boxill,

Fulton County Commissioner – District 6

AIR SYSTEMS HEATING & COOLING, INC.
SALES & SERVICE
SERVICING ALL BRANDS
Kelvinator
Heating and Cooling Products
3165 Washington St • P.O. Box 110
Covington, GA 30015
GA REG CL 300571
(770) 787-0602
(770) 787-8093 fax
Locally Owned & Operated
VISA

A M F
ATLANTA MICRO FUND
Have an existing business?
Always dreamed of owning your own business?
Receive the financial assistance you need to realize your entrepreneurial dreams!
To Learn More About Our Loan Program
Contact:
Marvin Bryant
Loan Fund Manager
678.539.6900

ATLANTA TECHNICAL COLLEGE
changes things.
One student at a time.
Are you ready to make a change?
Call Atlanta Tech at 404.225.4400.
Most Atlanta Tech students do not pay for tuition, thanks to the HOPE Grant.
www.atlantatech.edu
ATLANTA
TECHNICAL
COLLEGE

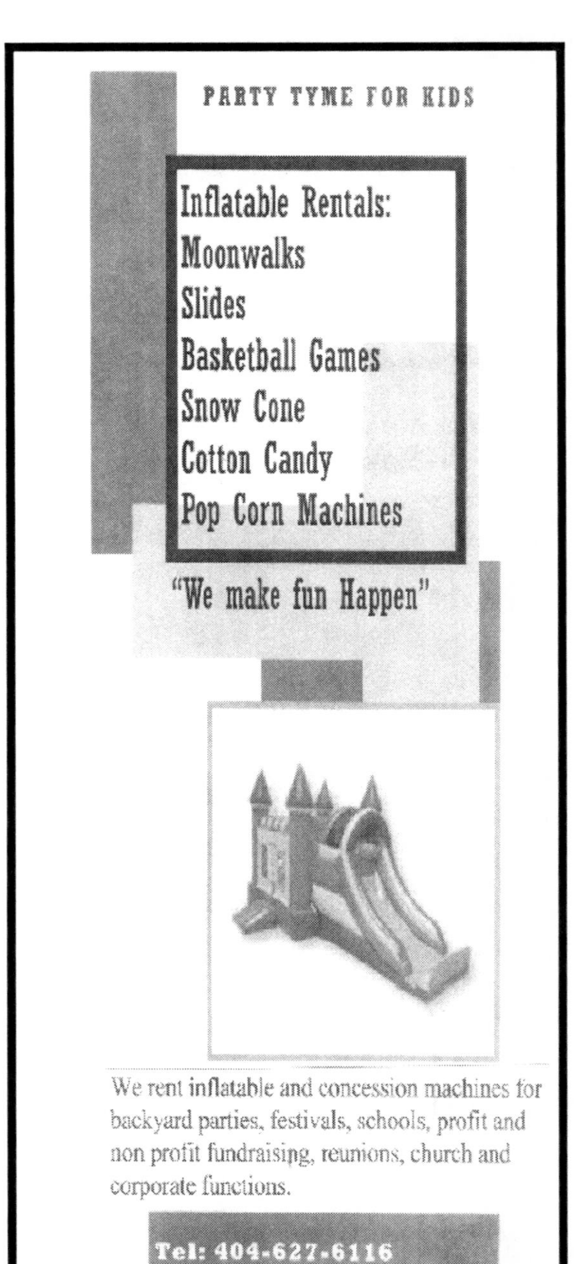
PARTY TYME FOR KIDS
Inflatable Rentals:
Moonwalks
Slides
Basketball Games
Snow Cone
Cotton Candy
Pop Corn Machines
"We make fun Happen"
We rent inflatable and concession machines for backyard parties, festivals, schools, profit and non profit fundraising, reunions, church and corporate functions.
Tel: 404-627-6116

Sharita Robinson, MS, PHR
sharitamr@bellsouth.net
404-551-5098

Services include:

Strategic Human Resources Planning
Career Transition & Individual Coaching

Personalized Poetry Gift Baskets

Wonderfully Made Creations
From NAJANIQUE
Naja Saleem, Founder
912-541-5328 najanique@mindspring.com
"When you can't find the words to say..."

Customized Cards Announcements

Virginia Green, P.C.
Certified Public Accountants

3360 Windsor Castle Court • Decatur, Georgia 30034
(770) 981-2470 • (770) 981-1847
email: vgreencpa@mindspring.com

"Your income is your credit"

Home Loans • Rent To Own • Lease Purchase
Pre-Foreclosure Assistance / Car Program Available

MICHELLE DAVIS
OFFICE: (770) 935-6257
FAX: (404) 766-2679

E-mail: michelledavis_hfm@yahoo.com
www.hfmexperience.org

3675 CRESTWOOD PARKWAY, SUITE 400 · DULUTH, GA 30096

Something Special Catering
A Cut Above The Rest

HOWARD E. MOYE

253 Covington Drive
Hiram, GA 30141
(770) 943-2828 (Home)
(404) 725-2520 (Cell)

Cell - 404-579-2279
Cell - 404-579-4225
Cell - 678-233-7311
Nextel - 155*132739*5

Christian Home Improvement

Residential & Commercial Repairs
Plumbing Specialist
"Get the Best for Less"

JEFF CHRISTIAN
Licensed Contractor
Lic.# 07-25887

Plumbing, Carpentry, Electrical
Flooring, Painting, Pressure Washing
and Much More...

BEATRICE BROWN

Senior Tax Preparer

770-256 6748

PRC Says Thanks To All Our Sponsors, Advertisers And Patrons!

PATRONS

Anita Anderson
Ariana Battle
Folyan Battle
Kim Billups
Linda Blash
Dalisa Boswell
Polly Boyd
Daniel Brown
Jacqueline Brown
Pat Brown
Sherise Brown
Louis Coleman
Douglas Curate
Bill Dennis
Helen J. DuBose
Brittany S. Evora
Stephanie Flowers
Ellen N. Fleming
Jayln N. Fleming
Waymon Fowler
Crystal Foster
Deon Franklin, Jr.
Kenneth J. Gaines
Freddy Garcia
Latoya Hicks Garcia
Pastor Kenneth Garian
Marion C. Gray, Sr.
Queen La'Rosa Green

Anna Hicks
Brian Hicks
Michael Hicks
Margaret P. Hooker
Fred Howard
Martha Hutchins
Jerome
June
Deidra Johnson
Khaleema
Travie Leslie
Chunda Lewis
Nequa Martin
Nicholas Martin
Demetria McAlpine
Keri McDonald
Ida G. McLaughlin
Bessie L. Mills
Douglas Moore
Wendy Scruggs-Murray
Peanut
Loretta Pitts
Chris Reese
Damarius Rivers
Shanteria Rivers
Tracy Rivers
Marvin/Royce Roberts
Diane Rutcin
Shirley Shephard
Brenda Shirley
Marilyn Simmons

Tayna Smith
Donald Stubbs
Yvonne Sumlin
Pamela Swain
Carvasdas Thomas
Malissa Tompkins
Roderick Walls
Thomas Walton
Dr. Alyce M. Ware
Kate Williams
Clarence Williams
Trina Williams
Yvonne Williams
Wash World
Samuel Wright

On behalf of the Peoplestown Revitalization Corporation, we would like to thank all of our contributors!

Autographs

Autographs

Special Notes

Special Notes

Who's Who In Peoplestown

Who's Who In Peoplestown

Printed in the United States
106522LV00001B/250-438/P